THIS BOOK IS FROM THE LIFE OF:

IT IS DEDICATED TO:

FOR OUR FAMILIES

I LIVED THIS

A WORKBOOK FOR WRITING YOUR LIFE STORY

WRITTEN BY YOU

WITH HELP FROM
JESSICA REEDER &
CHRISTINA ATKINS

ILIVEDTHIS.COM

For permission requests, write to the publisher at:
permissions@jhfearless.com

Get news and inspiration:
ILivedThis.com

ISBN-13: 978-1542682800
ISBN-10: 1542682800

TABLE OF CONTENTS

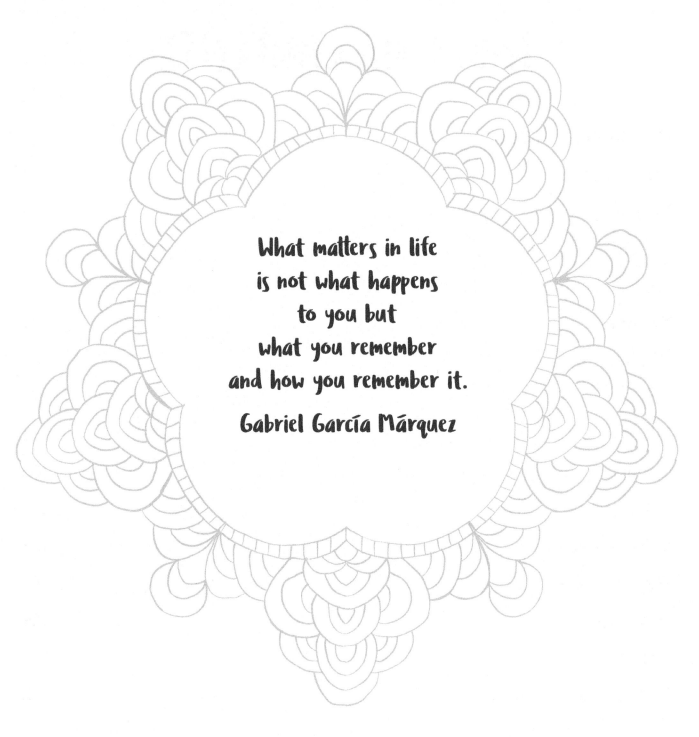

What matters in life
is not what happens
to you but
what you remember
and how you remember it.

Gabriel García Márquez

2

HOW TO USE THIS BOOK

This book will guide you through writing your life story as a memoir. It's not quite the same as an autobiography: you won't be asked about every detail of your life. Instead, it's about finding the story you wish to tell. What you want to say is up to you, but this book will give you some ideas.

Here's one idea: Imagine that the person reading this is a few generations into the future. They might know very little about you, your family, or this time in history. What would you like to tell that person?

Share your deep thoughts! If something has special meaning for you, explore it. Though you may want your book to be read by others, you can write it for yourself too. This might be an opportunity for you to look deeper at some of life's rarely-examined events and lessons.

Think about all the wisdom you've gained, and the battles you've fought to become the person you are. The important part of a life story goes beyond the facts; it's more about *who* you have become and *why*. In other words, details aren't always as important as the big picture. You lived through some interesting times, and you have a unique perspective on what that was like.

Be honest, even when it hurts or feels dangerous. We connect with each other through truth and storytelling, and your experiences may one day empower another person to face their own challenges.

This book assumes you're writing this as an older person, but you can use it at any stage of life. Simply fill out the sections that apply to you. Answer the questions you feel most strongly about, and skip the ones you don't have much to say about.

In fact, do whatever you want to transform this book into *your* book. Fill it out in whatever order you like. Skip sections. Make up your own questions. Color and draw in it. Rip out pages. Glue in photos.

Many people like to type their answers instead of writing by hand. If that works for you, just think of this book as a guide to get you started.

Or, if the structure here works for you, use it! Enjoy the process, and have fun writing your story.

Use these pages to draw your family tree.

4

For inspiration & ideas, turn to the next page.

DRAWING A FAMILY CHART

Modern families can be complicated. When it comes to drawing your own family "tree," use any method that makes sense for your own unique web of relationships and history.
Here are two of the most common types of family charts.

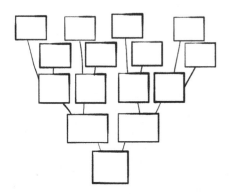

FAMILY TREE

This is the traditional, branching chart you may have seen. Start by writing your name at the bottom of the page. Add siblings' and cousins' names on the same line as your own. Then start a new row above, and fill in your parents' generation. Draw lines connecting people who are directly related (like you with your parents) or married.

Many people like to draw two trees: one expanding upward to show your ancestors, and one expanding downward for your descendants.

FAMILY FAN CHART

Larger, more complex family relationships may be easier to diagram in a fan chart. This is useful if you have lots of variation in your family structure!

Write your name at the center and expand the chart outward, with each row representing a separate generation. You can use the full 360 degrees to make a circle, if needed. Generally, your ancestors' names are written above your name, and descendants written below. Or make multiple charts, as needed!

Divide the rows so each box contains one name (e.g. if you have six kids, divide the row into six parts).

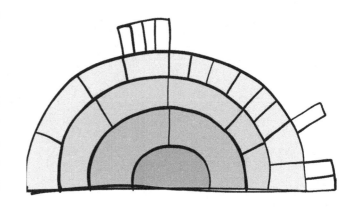

TIP: SKETCH YOUR CHART IN PENCIL FIRST!

To the best of your knowledge, where did your ancestors come from? Color, draw, or write on this map.

Are there certain cultures or regions that you identify with strongly?

....

....

....

....

....

What are your strongest memories of your grandparents and great-grandparents (if you knew them)?

Family is not an
important thing.
It's everything.
Michael J. Fox

9

Does your family have any unique or special genetic traits?

Are there certain traditions that are special to your family?

FROM THE KITCHEN OF: ....

PREP TIME: .... COOK TIME: .... SERVES: ....

INGREDIENTS: INSTRUCTIONS:

Close your eyes and picture your mother (or mother figure). Sketch her face, describe her, or add a photo here.

....

....

....

....

....

....

....

When you picture your mother (figure) at her happiest, what is she doing?
What are/were her talents and skills?

....

....

....

....

....

....

....

What do you know about her life story?

I remember my mother's prayers and they have always followed me. They have clung to me all my life.

Abraham Lincoln

Close your eyes and picture your father (or father figure). Sketch his face, describe him, or add a photo here.

....

....

....

....

....

....

....

When you picture your father (figure) at his happiest, what is he doing?
What are/were his talents and skills?

....

....

....

....

....

....

What do you know about his life story?

Being an old farm boy myself, chickens coming home to roost never did make me sad; they've always made me glad.

Malcolm X

What do you know about your parents' relationship?

....

....

....

....

....

....

....

Do you have siblings? Step-siblings? Where are they now?

....

....

....

....

....

....

....

Was there a significant event that affected your relationship with one or more of your family members?

WRITE YOUR STORY

Write more about your family background on these next pages.
Here are some questions to inspire you, or you can tell any story you think is important to share.

A few prompts:

What foods did your grandparents eat? What sort of clothes did they wear?
What else do you know about your grandparents' generation?
Did your parents and grandparents all get along?

What do/did you appreciate most about your mother?
What is/was hardest for you to overcome in your relationship with your mother?
What does/did your mother most want for you?
What do/did you most want for her?

What do/did you appreciate most about your father?
What is/was hardest for you to overcome in your relationship with your father?
What do/did your father most want for you?
What do/did you most want for him?

Did any sibling, cousin, or other person in your generation stand out for you as a special friend or ally?
Did you have any enemies among your siblings or cousins?

The bond that
links your true family
is not one of blood,
but of respect and joy
in each other's life.

Richard Bach

CHILDHOOD

I was born on:

_____

in the year:

_____

I turned 12 in the year:

_____

What is your earliest memory?

....

....

....

....

....

....

....

....

As a child, what was your favorite food?

....

....

....

What was your favorite toy, game, or pastime?

....

....

....

How would you describe your home life? What do you think made your home unique?

....

....

....

....

....

....

....

What did your house sound like? What did it smell like?

....

....

....

....

....

....

What do remember about the place(s) you lived up until the age of 12 or so?

....

....

....

....

....

....

....

....

What were the rules you were expected to follow?

....

....

....

....

....

....

....

Was there an important person in your childhood who had a big effect on you?

....

....

....

....

....

Do you remember any major historical events that happened while you were young?
How did these events affect you and your family or community?

....

....

....

....

....

....

....

....

....

There is always
one moment in
childhood when the
door opens and lets
the future in.
Graham Greene

What was your school like? What was it like to be in school?

....

....

....

....

....

....

....

....

....

....

....

....

....

....

....

If you have a picture
you like from school or
childhood, paste it here.

Who were the three most influential people in your childhood, positive or negative?
(e.g. parents, grandparents, teachers, role models, friends, siblings. . .) Why?

Adults are just obsolete children and the hell with them.

Dr. Seuss

29

WRITE YOUR STORY

Write more about your childhood on these next pages.
Here are some questions to inspire you, or tell the story you think is most important to share.

A few prompts:

Did you have a favorite pet as a young child?
Did you have a best friend (real or imaginary)?

What were you like as a child? Were you quiet? Active? Shy? Brave? Imaginative? Adventurous?
Tell a story of an event or experience that you will always remember from your childhood.

What was your school like?
What kind of student were you?
Did you have a favorite teacher? Why? How about a least favorite?
Who supported and encouraged you to do well in school, if anyone?

What was your neighborhood or community like?
Did you have any friends' houses you spent lots of time at?
What were your friends' houses like?

How did your family celebrate holidays?
How did you spend your summers?

If you carry
your childhood
with you, you never
become older.

Tom Stoppard

34

TEENAGE YEARS

I turned 13 in _____

I turned 19 in _____

Picture yourself at thirteen, and again at nineteen. How did you change?

If you have a photo you like from your teenage years, paste it here.

What was going on in the world during those years?

What was going on in your family during those years?

How did the events going on around you affect you personally?

_____

_____

_____

_____

_____

_____

_____

_____

_____

_____

_____

_____

_____

_____

What was your personality like as a teenager?

....

....

....

....

....

....

....

What social groups did you hang around with? Did you feel accepted?

....

....

....

....

....

....

....

Find out who you are
and be that person ...
live that truth and
everything else
will come.

Ellen DeGeneres

Tell a story about an event or experience you'll always remember from your teenage years.

What did you struggle with in these years? What were you good at?

Identity is a prison you can never escape, but the way to redeem your past is not to run from it, but to try to understand it.

Jay-Z

If you could write a note to your teenaged self, what would you say?

What were your top five bands or musical artists? Why?

And these children
that you spit on
as they try to
change their worlds
are immune to
your consultations
They're quite aware
of what they're
going through...
David Bowie

WRITE YOUR STORY

Write more about your teenage years on these next pages.
Here are some questions to inspire you, or tell the story you think is most important to share.

A few prompts:

What did you do for fun as a teenager?
Where did you spend most of your time?

Did you fall in love as a teenager?
Was there a time when you felt you had lost a little of your innocence?

Did you start to have an idea about what you wanted your future to be like?
Who were some of the people that affected your life during these years? Friends, family, teachers?
Did one person stand out in particular?

What role did school play in your life?
What activities were you involved in at school?
Did you have any favorite classes, or classes you hated? Why?

When you turned 18, what were your thoughts about being a legal adult?
Did you make any big life changes when you turned 18?

All teenagers
have this desire to
somehow run away.

Joan Chen

TWENTIES

I turned 20 in:

I turned 29 in:

49

Picture yourself at twenty, and again at twenty-nine. How did you change?

....

....

....

....

....

....

....

What was going on in the world during your twenties?

....

....

....

....

....

....

....

What was going on in your family in these years?

....

....

....

....

....

....

....

Did you go through significant life changes (moving, new job, marriage, kids...) during these years?

....

....

....

....

....

....

....

How did all these events affect you personally?

....

....

....

....

....

....

....

....

....

....

....

....

....

....

....

....

....

What did you do for work in your twenties?

....

....

....

....

....

What did you do for fun?

....

....

....

....

....

....

....

....

What sorts of things were trendy or in style at the time? How did you feel about pop culture?

....

....

....

....

....

....

....

If you have a picture you like from
your twenties, paste it here.

Did you make any major and/or difficult decisions during these years?

....

....

....

....

....

....

....

....

Would you make the same choice again?

....

....

....

....

Live as if you were
to die tomorrow.
Learn as if you
were to live forever.
Mahatma Gandhi

....

Describe an event or experience from your twenties that you'll always remember.

Describe the best shows (concerts, plays, movies...) you saw in your twenties. What made them special?

All of us get lost in the darkness, dreamers learn to steer by the stars.
Rush

WRITE YOUR STORY

Write more about your twenties on these next pages.
Here are some questions to inspire you, or tell the story you think is most important to share.

A few prompts:

What did you do for your 21st birthday?

What did you do on a normal Saturday night?

Did you start feeling like a grownup in these years? Why or why not?

Who were the most influential people in your life during these years?

What were your feelings about dating, marriage and children in your twenties?

What was your greatest ambition?

What was your personal style?

Did you belong to any subcultures, circles or clubs?

What were you excited about learning during your twenties?

Did you have an idea of what your career or life path would be?

59

Tell him yes.
Even if you are dying of
fear, even if you are
sorry later, because
whatever you do, you will
be sorry all the rest of
your life if you say no.
Gabriel García
Márquez

THIRTIES

I turned 30 in

I turned 39 in

63

Picture yourself at thirty, and again at thirty-nine. How did you change?

....

....

....

....

....

....

....

What was going on in the world during your thirties?

....

....

....

....

....

....

....

What was going on in your family in these years?

....

....

....

....

....

....

Did you go through significant life changes (moving, new job, marriage, kids...)?

....

....

....

....

....

....

How did all these events affect you personally?

Did any of your beliefs (about politics, culture, spirituality...) start to change in your thirties? How?

As you enter positions
of trust and power,
dream a little
before you think.
Toni Morrison

Who were the most influential people in your life at this time?

....
....
....
....
....

What made these relationships so special?

....
....
....
....
....
....
....
....

Describe the 3-5 things you're most proud of accomplishing in your thirties. Why?

It takes a long time to get to be a diva. I mean, you gotta work at it.

Diana Ross

Describe your community in those years: your town, your neighborhood, or your friends and family.

....

....

....

....

....

....

....

If you have a picture you like from
your thirties, paste it here.

....

....

....

....

....

....

....

....

....

What did you do for work (including housework)? What did you do for fun?

WRITE YOUR STORY

Write more about your thirties on these next pages.
Here are some questions to inspire you, or tell the story you think is most important to share.

A few prompts:
Did you make any major choices or decisions during these years?
Would you make the same choice again?

Did you have any special hobbies or activities?

When did you start to feel like you really knew yourself?

Did your relationship with your parents or other family members change during these years?

Did you start seeing yourself as a "grownup"? Why and how?

How did you feel about the politics of the time?
Did you have any unpopular opinions (political or otherwise)? Why?

Did you form any special connections with neighbors or community members?

74

She discovered
with great delight
that one does not love one's
children just because they are
one's children, but because
of the friendship formed
while raising them.

Gabriel García
Márquez

75

FORTIES

_____

to

_____

Picture yourself at forty, and again at forty-nine. How did you change?

....

....

....

....

....

....

....

....

What was going on in the world during your forties?

....

....

....

....

....

....

....

....

What was going on in your family in these years?

....

....

....

....

....

....

....

Did you go through significant life changes (moving, new job, marriage, kids...)?

....

....

....

....

....

....

....

....

How did all these events affect you personally?

....

....

....

....

....

....

....

....

....

....

....

....

....

....

....

What were a few of your proudest moments during your forties? What made these moments special?

The body is
at its best between
the ages of thirty and
thirty-five; the mind is
at its best about the
age of forty-nine.

Aristotle

Describe a typical day in your forties. Where did you live?
How did you spend your time? How did you feel?

If you have a picture you like
from your forties, paste it here.

Did you start to gain a sense of what you wanted to accomplish
in your life? What were your goals at this time?

Learn from yesterday,
live for today, hope
for tomorrow. The
important thing is not
to stop questioning.

Albert Einstein

Tell a story of an event or experience from your forties that you will always remember.

Who were the closest people in your life during your forties? Did you develop any unique relationships?

Walking with a friend in the dark is better than walking alone in the light.

Helen Keller

WRITE YOUR STORY

Write more about your forties on these next pages.
Here are some questions to inspire you, or tell the story you think is most important to share.

A few prompts:

Who were the most influential people in your life during these years?

What was your relationship with faith and spirituality?

Did you keep up with popular culture, or did you move away from it?

Did you go through any hard times during these years?

What gave you hope when things seemed most difficult?

Did your perception of yourself change in these years?

Did you consider going back to school or taking up a new profession?

Did you make any major choices or decisions?
Would you make the same choice(s) again?

Middle age is when
you're sitting at home
on a Saturday night
and the telephone rings
and you hope it isn't
for you.
Ogden Nash

FIFTIES

_____ to _____

Picture yourself at fifty, and again at fifty-nine. How did you change?

....

....

....

....

....

....

....

What was going on in the world during your fifties?

....

....

....

....

....

....

....

....

What was going on in your family in these years?

....

....

....

....

....

....

....

Did you go through significant life changes?

....

....

....

....

....

....

....

How did all these events affect you personally?

Did you notice changes in your close friendships and family relationships around this time?

What did you miss about being younger?

....

....

....

....

....

....

....

What did you like about getting older?

....

....

....

....

....

....

....

What were your career and life goals at this time? Was your perspective on these things changing?

We never really
grow up, we only
learn how to act
in public.
Bryan White

97

What did you do in your free time in these years? Did you have a particular project that was special?

....

....

....

....

....

....

....

....

If you have a picture you like
from your fifties, paste it here.

....

....

....

....

....

....

....

....

....

What were your biggest influences during your fifties? Who and what were you excited about?

Yesterday I was
clever, so I wanted
to change the world.
Today I am wise, so I
am changing myself.

Rumi

WRITE YOUR STORY

Write more about your fifties on these next pages.
Here are some questions to inspire you, or tell the story you think is most important to share.

A few prompts:

Who were the most influential people in your life during these years?

Tell a story of an event or experience that you will always remember from your fifties.

Did you make any major choices or decisions during these years?
Would you make the same choice again?

Did you keep in touch (or get back in touch) with people from your younger years?
What was that like?

What was a typical day like during your fifties?

What did you do for entertainment?

What was your personal style in these years?

I have a rule: If the temperature is less than my age, I don't get out of bed.

Ellen DeGeneres

SIXTIES

_____

to

_____

Picture yourself at sixty, and again at sixty-nine. How did you change?

....

....

....

....

....

....

....

What was going on in the world during your sixties?

....

....

....

....

....

....

....

....

What was going on in your family in these years?

Did you go through significant life changes?

How did all these events affect you personally?

....

....

....

....

....

....

....

....

....

....

....

....

....

....

....

How did it feel to watch the young people in your family become adults and build their own lives?

I have learned
that to be
with those I like
is enough.
Walt Whitman

Tell a story of an event or experience that you will always remember from your sixties.

If you have a picture you like
from your sixties, paste it here.

What foods, music, books, and entertainment were you into? Did you find your tastes had evolved?

If you always do
what interests you,
at least one person
is pleased.
Katharine Hepburn

What did you worry about during these years?

....

....

....

....

....

....

....

What were you excited or happy about?

....

....

....

....

....

....

....

How did you start planning for the "golden years" ahead? What was important in this process?

Though no one can go back and make a brand-new start, anyone can start from now and make a brand-new ending.

Carl Bard

WRITE YOUR STORY

Write more about your sixties on these next pages.
Here are some questions to inspire you, or tell the story you think is most important to share.

A few prompts:

If you were working, did you start thinking about retirement?
What factors affected that decision?

What was a typical day like during your sixties?

Did you reach a point in these years where you felt you truly knew yourself?

Did you start to feel younger in your mind than in your body?

Did you try (and like) something you never would have tried as a younger person?

Did you make any major choices or decisions during these years?
Would you make the same choice again?

Who were the most influential people in your life during these years?

Someone is sitting
in the shade today
because someone
planted a tree
a long time ago.

Warren Buffett

SEVENTIES

_____ to _____

Picture yourself at seventy, and again at seventy-nine. How did you change?

....

....

....

....

....

....

....

What was going on in the world during your seventies?

....

....

....

....

....

....

....

....

What was going on in your family in these years?

....

....

....

....

....

....

....

Did you go through significant life changes?

....

....

....

....

....

....

....

How did all of these events affect you personally?

....

....

....

....

....

....

....

....

....

....

....

....

Did you start to feel you had gained some true wisdom over the years?
What were your big realizations and why?

No matter what, nobody can take away the dances you've already had.

Gabriel García Márquez

How did it feel to turn 70? How did you celebrate that birthday?

....

....

....

....

....

....

....

If you have a picture you like from
your seventies, paste it here.

What did you think about the politics of the time?

....

....

....

....

....

....

....

Did you see any history repeat itself?

....

....

....

....

....

....

....

Did you let go of any old beliefs, fears, or habits? What were they, and how did you change your mind?

What were your favorite traditions (with family, friends, or community) during these years?

....

....

....

....

....

....

....

....

....

....

....

The more you
praise and celebrate
your life, the more
there is in life to
celebrate.

Oprah Winfrey

WRITE YOUR STORY

Write more about your seventies on these next pages.
Here are some questions to inspire you, or tell the story you think is most important to share.

A few prompts:

What was a typical day like during your seventies?

Did you pick up a new hobby or pastime in these years?

How did you feel about the youth culture of the time?

What did you learn from your children and grandchildren's experiences?

Who were the most influential people in your life during these years?
What were your favorite traditions during this time?

Did you make any major choices or decisions during these years?
Would you make the same choice again?

Tell a story of an event or experience that you will always remember from your seventies.

To be seventy years young is sometimes far more cheerful and hopeful than to be forty years old.

Oliver Wendell Holmes

EIGHTIES & NINETIES

_____

to

_____

What is happening in the world now? What are your opinions on current events and culture?

What is happening in your family or community?

....

....

....

....

....

....

....

....

Where do you live now? Have you moved since your 80th birthday?

....

....

....

....

....

Describe a moment in recent years when you truly felt proud of your life and accomplishments.

....
....
....
....
....
....
....

If you have a picture you like from
recent years, paste it here.

....
....
....
....
....
....
....
....
....

Have you made any big or difficult choices since turning 80? What did you choose and why?

The longer I live,
the more beautiful
life becomes.
Frank Lloyd Wright

Who are you closest with in your life now?

....

....

....

....

....

....

....

What interests, activities, and hobbies have you kept up with all these years? What have you dropped?

....

....

....

....

....

....

....

....

Have any of your views on life changed recently? What changed, and why?

....

....

....

....

....

....

....

Do you have beliefs that you wish the rest of the world shared? What are they, and why?

....

....

....

....

....

....

....

WRITE YOUR STORY

Write more about your eighties and nineties on these next pages.
Here are some questions to inspire you, or tell the story you think is most important to share.

A few prompts:

What was a typical day like during your eighties?
What about your nineties?

How have you changed as a person during these years?

How has your relationship with your loved ones changed?

What music do you listen to recently?

Have you made any new friends or reconnected with old ones?

What do you miss (foods, music, activities, people...) about the old times?

What is better now than it was when you were young?

Tomorrow hopes
we have learned
something from
yesterday.
John Wayne

THE BIG PICTURE

What big changes have you seen in the world since you were a child? What do they mean to you?

Looking back at the major historical events you lived through, were any of them more (or less) important than you thought at the time? Why and how?

We are not
makers of history.
We are made
by history.
Martin Luther
King, Jr.

Looking back, what were some big turning points in your life? Do you see those times differently now?

What's one thing that happened in your lifetime that you would never have thought was possible?

If you could change one thing about the world, what would it be?

If you could change one thing about your life, what would it be?

Do you have any messages to the people who might be reading this book?

....

....

....

....

....

....

....

....

....

....

....

....

....

There are a
thousand ways to
kneel and kiss the
ground; there are
a thousand ways
to go home again.

Rumi

Fill this space with a few photos or sketches
of important things, people, or memories.

Fill this space with a few photos or sketches
of important things, people, or memories.

WRITE YOUR STORY

Write more about your life and thoughts on these next pages.
Here are some questions to inspire you, or tell the story you think is most important to share.

A few prompts:

How does it feel to write about your life?

If you could go back and do anything differently, what would it be?

What have you learned that you wish everybody understood?

What do you worry about?
What fears have you let go?

What are you excited about?

What makes you feel joyful, peaceful, or just plain happy?

What is your feeling about God, faith, spirituality, religion, magic... the sublime?

What will be the date of your hundredth birthday?
What do you think about turning 100?

Good friends,
good books, and a
sleepy conscience:
this is the ideal life.
Mark Twain

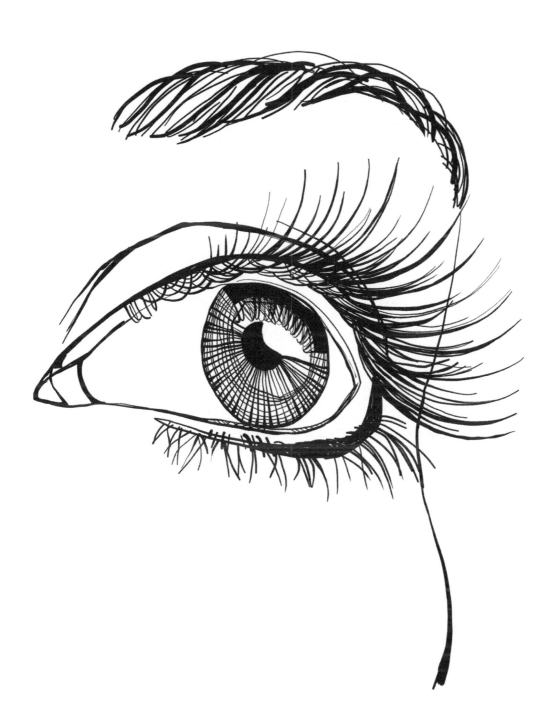

NOTE
TO
SELF

What's something you always meant to do, but haven't gotten around to?

....
....
....
....
....
....
....

Anything you want to try in the next few years?

....
....
....
....
....
....
....

What's on your bucket list? (If you don't have one, make it now!)

A man is a success
if he gets up in the
morning and goes to
bed at night and in
between does what he
wants to do.
Bob Dylan

161

Have you realized anything important in the course of writing this book?

Write a note to yourself or a loved one, to read in five years.
Don't forget to mark your calendar to come back and read it later!

The final forming
of a person's
character lies in
their own hands.

Anne Frank

WRITE YOUR STORY

This is it! The end of the book. Congratulations on getting this far.

Now is your moment to finish saying anything you still want to say.

Did the questions skip something very important to you?

Did you realize something you'd like to share?

Or do you just have more to tell?

Fill these final pages however you like: with writing, sketches, photos, memorabilia... whatever.

Or, if you have nothing left to say about yourself, write a note to somebody else.

(Or just leave it blank!)

This is your book. How do you want to finish it?

The secret to life
is meaningless
unless you
discover it
yourself.

W. Somerset
Maugham

No matter how
difficult and painful
it may be, nothing
sounds as good
to the soul
as the truth.

Martha Beck

THE SECRET

If there's something you've been holding on to, and you'd like somebody to know about it in the future, you can put it here.

Write it down on a separate piece of paper, seal it in an envelope, and write on the envelope when you want it to be opened and by whom.

Tuck the envelope in here for safekeeping.

If you're reading this book and you are/were close to its author, use this space to add your own reactions and reflections. Or just write a note to the author.

FAMILY & FRIENDS' NOTES

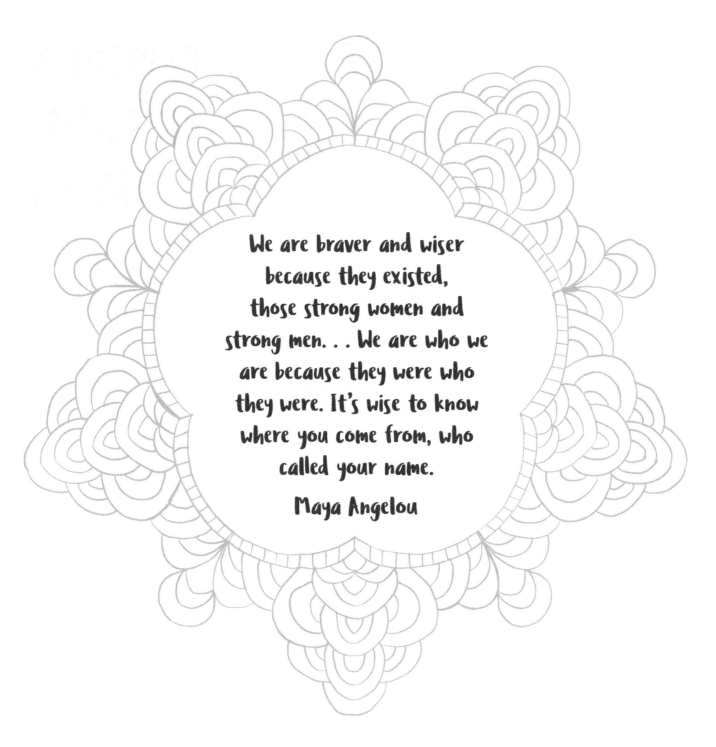

We are braver and wiser
because they existed,
those strong women and
strong men. . . We are who we
are because they were who
they were. It's wise to know
where you come from, who
called your name.

Maya Angelou

GET HELP, IDEAS & SUPPORT: JOIN US ONLINE!

Hey! We're online and we're building a community of people who are writing their life stories. We would love to have you join us. Here are a few places you can connect with us and other storytellers:

FACEBOOK
HTTP://FACEBOOK.COM/GROUPS/ILIVEDTHIS

Join our Facebook group for people who are using this workbook to write their own stories.
We're there most days, with prompts and ideas to spark your memory.
If you have questions or challenges, this is a great place to talk about them.

WEBSITE
HTTP://ILIVEDTHIS.COM

We're updating our website and blog with tips and strategies for writing your own life story.
Plus, you can find out what's new with the book (and if it's going on sale soon!)
From our website, you can also sign up for email updates.
Or, send us a message using the contact form.
We love to hear from you.

Happy writing!

- JESSICA & CHRISTINA

ABOUT THE AUTHORS

JESSICA REEDER

JESSICAREEDER.COM

Jessica is a writer, ghostwriter, and editor specializing in helping people write their memoirs and life stories. She is inspired by art, creativity, truth, and beauty. Jessica lives in the Sierras with her partner David, their dog Spencer, and their cat Ozymandias, King of Kings.

CHRISTINA ATKINS

CHAOSTINA.COM

Christina is a compulsive creative, illustrator, writer, and crafter. She is currently writing and illustrating her first solo fiction novel. Christina lives in the Washington, DC area with her husband, son, and feisty cairn terrier, but she originates from the red hills of Utah and still calls the desert home.

Made in the USA
Monee, IL
21 April 2020